I AND THE VILLAGE

The publishers gratefully acknowledge the financial assistance of the Arts Council/An Chomhairle Ealaíon

First published in 2002 by Marino Books
16 Hume Street Dublin 2
Tel: (01) 661 5299; Fax: (01) 661 8583
E.mail: books@marino.ie
An imprint of Mercier Press
Website: www.mercier.ie

Trade enquiries to CMD Distribution
55A Spruce Avenue
Stillorgan Industrial Park
Blackrock County Dublin
Tel: (01) 294 2560; Fax: (01) 294 2565
E.mail: cmd@columba.ie

© Gabriel Fitzmaurice 2002

ISBN 1 86023 149 7
10 9 8 7 6 5 4 3 2 1

A CIP record for this title is available
from the British Library

Cover design by Marino Books
Cover illustration courtesy of the
Museum of Modern Art, New York

Printed in Ireland by ColourBooks,
Baldoyle Industrial Estate, Dublin 13

I AND THE VILLAGE

GABRIEL FITZMAURICE

Praise for A Wrenboy's Carnival

'Fitzmaurice is a wonderful poet . . . A moving and thought-provoking collection.'

GILES FODEN, THE GUARDIAN

'Not unlike those of Goldsmith and Burns, these poems are endowed with charm, wit and generosity of spirit . . . He transcends sentimentality to effect what that redoubtable school inspector Matthew Arnold would recognise as "a criticism of life" . . . His elegies and love poems are direct, moving evocations; his poems to and about friends and neighbours will make you wish you were among them.'

JAMES J. MCAULEY, THE IRISH TIMES

'Gabriel Fitzmaurice has demonstrated time and again that Moyvane, County Kerry, his heartland, is one of the global villages of our day . . . There is a deceptive ease to much of his work. This volume shows a spirited voice at work that is able to preserve the grain of Irish folklore in modern verse, to translate in a clear, rhythmic idiom and to look with a wise eye at the local harmonies we make of our heroes, daily routines, moments of vision, family and village life.'

BRIAN COATES, POETRY IRELAND REVIEW

'Simplicity can be the height of perfection? If so, there is a dash of both here.'

BOOKS IRELAND

OTHER BOOKS BY GABRIEL FITZMAURICE

POETRY

Rainsong (Beaver Row Press, Dublin, 1984)

Road to the Horizon (Beaver Row Press, 1987)

Dancing Through (Beaver Row Press, 1990)

The Father's Part (Story Line Press, Oregon, 1992)

The Space Between: New and Selected Poems, 1984-1992
　(Cló Iar-Chonnachta, Conamara, 1993)

The Village Sings (Story Line Press, Cló Iar-Chonnachta,
　Peterloo Poets, Cornwall, 1996)

A Wrenboy's Carnival: Poems, 1980–2000 (Wolfhound
　Press, Dublin, Peterloo Poets, 2000)

Nocht (Coiscéim, Dublin, 1989)

Ag Síobshiúl Chun An Rince (Coiscéim, 1995)

Giolla na nAmhrán: Dánta 1988–1998 (Coiscéim, 1998)

CHILDREN'S POETRY

The Moving Stair (The *Kerryman*, Tralee, 1989)

The Moving Stair (Poolbeg Press, Dublin, 1993)

But Dad! (Poolbeg Press, 1995)

Puppy and the Sausage (Poolbeg Press, 1998)

Dear Grandad (Poolbeg Press, 2001)

Nach Iontach Mar Atá (Cló Iar-Chonnachta, 1994)

ESSAYS

Kerry on My Mind (Salmon Publishing, Cliffs of Moher, 1999)

TRANSLATIONS

The Purge – A translation of An *Phurgóid* by Mícheál Ó
　hAirtnéide (Beaver Row Press, 1989)

Poems I Wish I'd Written – Translations from the Irish (Cló Iar-Chonnachta, 1996)

The Rhino's Specs/Spéaclaí an tSrónbheannaigh – Selected children's poems of Gabriel Rosenstock (Mercier Press, Dublin & Cork, 2002)

AS EDITOR

The Flowering Tree/An Crann Faoi Bhláth (contemporary poetry in Irish with verse translations) with Declan Kiberd (Wolfhound Press, 1991)

Between the Hills and Sea: Songs and Ballads of Kerry (Oidhreacht, Ballyheigue, 1991)

Con Greaney: Traditional Singer (Oidhreacht, 1991)

Homecoming/An Bealach 'na Bhaile (selected poems of Cathal Ó Searcaigh) (Cló Iar-Chonnachta, 1993)

Irish Poetry Now: Other Voices (Wolfhound Press, 1993)

Kerry Through Its Writers (New Island Books, Dublin, 1993)

The Listowel Literary Phenomenon: North Kerry Writers – A Critical Introduction (Cló Iar-Chonnachta, 1994)

Rusty Nails and Astronauts: A Wolfhound Poetry Anthology, with Robert Dunbar (Wolfhound Press, 1999)

'The Boro' and 'The Cross': The Parish of Moyvane–Knockanure, with Áine Cronin and John Looney (The Moyvane–Knockanure Millennium Book Committee, 2000)

The Kerry Anthology (Marino Books, Dublin, 2000)

Acknowledgements

Acknowledgements are due to the following, where many of the poems in this book first appeared: *A Conversation Piece: Poetry and Art* (Abbey Press/Ulster Museum), *An Ríocht*, *Birdsuit* (UK), *Breacadh*, *Hellas* (US), *Latitude* (Oxford University Press), *Podium*, *Poetry Ireland Review*, *Quadrant* (Australia), the *Formalist* (US), the *Lyric* (US), the *New Writer* (UK), *THE SHOp*; and to Lyric FM and Radio Kerry, where a number of them were first broadcast.

The publishers would like to thank the following for granting permission to reproduce copyright material: Caoimhín Ó Marcaigh for *'Oíche Nollaig na mBan'* ('The Women's Christmas Eve') by Seán Ó Ríordáin, originally published in *Eireaball Spideoige*, and Cló Iar-Chonnachta for *'An Bealach nach bhFilleann'* ('The Road of No Returning') and *'Amhrán'* ('Song'), by Cathal Ó Searcaigh, originally published in *Ag Tnúth leis an tSolas*.

In memory of my father and mother,
Jack and Maud Fitzmaurice,
and especially for Brenda, John and Nessa,
with love

Contents

3

1

AISLING GHEAL

One day back in the 'sixties
When everyone thought they were free
(Nothing that couldn't be done then) –
Everyone, that is, but me,

I was hitching a ride to the city
When a Zephyr pulled up by my side
And a vision in blonde hair and miniskirt
Asked me did I want a ride.

I sat into the Zephyr beside her,
And, struck by her beauty, I fell
Silent beside my fast driver,
Rehearsing what story to tell.

Would I talk of the Stones and the Beatles
And win her with music and lore
That I'd read up last week in the *Spotlight*,
Such tales as she'd want to hear more?

But what if she didn't like music?
What would we talk about then?
She talked of the troubles of Ireland
And the woes of her women and men;

And how England, that chauvinist England,
Was the cause of her trouble, but she
Would fight to the death for her freedom
And was counting on young men like me.

So I started to talk about England
But she railed they were barbarous boors
With no culture that any could speak of –
At least, no great culture like hers.

And she spoke of the Island of Scholars
And Saints who brought Europe to light,
And the chieftains and kings of Old Ireland
As eager in love as to fight;

And her poets who could charm with their verses,
And her bards who could soothe with their song,
And how England, that chauvinist England,
Had inflicted on her a great wrong.

And here was I squirming beside her,
Her miniskirt driving me wild,
Torn between acquiescing
(For I was but lately a child)

And protesting the glories of England
(For, alas, I had read history),
Afraid that this beautiful vision
Would vanish forever from me.

Yes! I spoke of the glories of England,
And she with a toss of her head
Cut off my history lesson:
'To hell with the Romans,' she said.

'To hell with the Romans,' she countered,
A beauty dismissing my suit,
And she dropped me off in the city
With my books, and the Romans, and truth.

And as she drove towards the horizon,
I knew I could never be free,
For in dreams she'd return to haunt me –
A marriage that never could be.

Now all I have left is this vision,
A beauty dismissing my suit,
A loss I have chosen to live with
With my books, and the Romans, and truth.

Aisling Gheal: 'a bright vision'. During the eighteenth and nineteenth centuries, some of our most powerful poems belong to the *aisling* type: political poems in which the poet encounters a vision-woman of great beauty, the spirit of Ireland, who foretells the coming of a Stuart redeemer.

To My D-28

Your body's unblemished
And sweetly you're strung,
A beauty I dreamed of
Since I was young,
But I'm middle-aged,
Losing hair, overweight,
And it's now you come to me,
My D-28.

As youngsters we dreamed
And talked of guitars,
We played out our crushes
On prized Yamahas,
And though we made music
When out on a date
We wished we were playing
A D-28.

We played Epiphones, Yamahas,
Fenders – all good;
We played on them music
To suit every mood.
But deep down we dreamed
That sooner or late
We'd all find our very own
D-28.

The past becomes present,
The dream becomes true.
It was music I loved, dear
(I thought it was you);
You're all that I dreamed of
But now it's too late,
For I'm pledged to another,
My D-28.

And still we make music
But now we both know
That there's no going back
To the long, long ago,
For my road is taken,
I'm resigned to my fate,
My first and forever
D-28.

FACING THE MUSIC

Joe Cooley, dying, takes his box again,
Plays for all who'll hear in Peterswell.
It's time to face the music, come what pain.

The pub's so thronged that some stand in the rain –
They've gathered here so that years hence they'll tell
How Cooley, dying, takes his box again.

Bound to him, though not by any chain,
Now they know how living can compel
A man to face the music, come what pain.

Faces pressed to the dripping window-pane,
We look at what in fear we try to quell,
As Cooley, dying, takes his box again.

He plays himself; his strength ebbs with the strain –
We know Joe knows he's playing his death knell.
It's time to face the music, come what pain,

We know that, here, deception is in vain
As, deliberate as a villanelle,
Joe Cooley, dying, takes his box again.
It's time to face the music, come what pain.

Box: a musicians' name for a button accordion

THE BALLAD OF JOE FITZMAURICE

The phonecall came from Uncle Mick
To hurry to Tralee,
The hospital had phoned him
And he needed me.

The hospital had told him
That Joe was close to death
And I should go to be with him
His last few hours on earth.

In Annagh Ward on Level Two
The matron said to me,
'Your uncle took a sudden turn,
He's very weak;

If anyone needs to see him,
Go to the phone and call.
There might be no tomorrow,
Though I don't have a crystal ball.'

And in I go to Uncle Joe,
Who thinks that I'm a nurse;
And I have seen my people die,
But this time it's worse:

Joe writhing on the pillow,
On the verge of sense,
Aware that he is dying,
Terrified and tense.

I pray that he'll die easy
As I hold his hand,
And the chaplain comes and prays with him
And he seems to understand.

'Hail Mary' – still he knows it –
He prays along with her,
And when the prayer is over
He makes a little stir.

'It's all right, Joe,' she soothes him,
'You're in Our Lady's care',
And she holds his hand and rubs
What's left of uncle's hair.

'I want, I want, I want,' he cries,
Tugging at his clothes.
'Our Lady will look after you,'
The chaplain calmly goes.
'I want, I want, I want,' he cries,
'I want to blow my nose.'

The chaplain takes her leave of us
But Joe can find no sleep:
'Hail Mary,' 'Holy Mary',
'Hail Mary', he repeats.

And this is all that's left him
On the edge of consciousness –
A prayer taught by his mother
To ease his last distress.

I join in the Hail Mary
So he'll know he's not alone,
Then hold his hand and rub his hair
And go out to the phone.

FATHER TOMMY'S LEAVING

Father Tommy's leaving. He has lost
Belief in what he lived for years ago.
Jesus doesn't answer from the Cross.

No more will he be compromised and crossed
By a Church that won't allow a priest to grow.
Father Tommy's leaving. He has lost

Belief. As he puts away the Host,
There's no one he can turn to. And no!
Jesus doesn't answer from the Cross.

Should he play it safe and never count the cost
Or stand up for his vision, blow by blow?
Father Tommy's leaving. He has lost

Belief. Yet loath to leave, he's tossed
Between himself or to uphold the status quo.
Jesus doesn't answer from the Cross.

A heart that once was burning turns to frost,
A Sacred Heart whose lamp has ceased to glow.
Father Tommy's leaving. He has lost.
Jesus doesn't answer from the Cross.

He Barks at His Own Echo

He barks at his own echo
All day and all night long;
He barks at his own echo,
He thinks he's not alone.

He barks at his own echo
And the echo answers back;
Whether he knows who's barking,
It still is good to bark.

Whether he knows who's barking,
It still is good to bark.

The *Díseart*

A sign points to the *Díseart*,
A place of prayer and art,
An empty convent chapel
Whose private Harry Clarkes

(Twelve stained-glass lancet windows)
Are public here today;
And some come here for beauty,
And some come here to pray.

Once I prayed in beauty
In the sanctuary of art –
How much was self-deception?
What now is Harry Clarke?

What signifies the light
That's filtered in this place?
In this convent chapel,
For some it still means grace.

But I leave the chapel,
It's given me no peace
(I'm through with self-deception),
Face the teeming streets.

Nothing was transfigured
But I saw things in his light,
A beauty not sufficient
To transform my plight.

And yet, the heavens streaming
Through windows stained to art
Illuminate the darkness
In the chapel of my heart.

Díseart: a retreat, a hermitage; a deserted place, a desert.
The *Díseart* is also a cultural and educational centre in
Dingle, County Kerry.
Harry Clarke (1889–1931) was Ireland's outstanding
stained-glass artist.

Heroes

Maybe there are no heroes –
Just people that we cheer
In our need for glory,
Born of our fear.

And the heroes we are cheering
Are much the same as we,
As fear of being nothing
Is changed to poetry.

THE BALLAD OF LONG JOHN BUTLER

Long John Butler was a rake
Who lived outside Knockray,
Drew the dole and never worked.
See him every day

On the same stool in Moss White's,
Knocking back his dole
In pints and whiskies at the bar,
Until one day he's told

By Bess, the woman of the house,
That he owes her sixty quid,
That he'll get no more liquor there
Until he pays the bill.

So Long John Butler leaves Moss White's
For exile down the street;
A refugee in Buckley's Bar,
He drinks there for a week,

A month, a season,
Stays out from Moss White's.
(It's not Moss White he's boycotting
But the wife.)

Time moves on; one evening
In September in Knockray,
Moss White slips into Buckley's Bar –
At the races all the day,

He won't go home till closing time,
He'll drink in every bar
And stand to the house in every pub.
(It wins him customers.)

As he stands to the crowd in Buckley's
He sees John Butler there,
Sidles over to him,
Making sure no one can hear.

'How's John Butler?' Moss salutes,
Slips him sixty quid
And tells him to go up to Bess
And pay the bill.

Long John Butler leaves the pub,
Returns to Moss White's
And says he's come to pay the bill,
That it's long been on his mind.

He hands two twenties to Bess White,
Who can't believe her luck:
She never thought John Butler
Would settle up.

Forty quid – just think of it!
Though it's not the full amount,
She writes off the remainder
And stands Long John a pint.

And Long John Butler drinks it
And spends the twenty more
In Moss White's that very night,
And now a customer

On the stool again where he belongs,
He drinks his dole by day,
As life gets back to normal
In Moss White's in Knockray.

At the Car Wash

The things we take for granted!
Take the washing of a car –
Take Frank Burke this morning
In the family gar-

age: I asked him for a car wash,
And he, in cleaning it,
Revealed himself in washing
As he scrubbed the mud and grit.

Most people when they wash a car
Take care with the parts you see:
They're the superficial ones.
But the ones who care beneath,

Knowing 'twill soon return again
To its former state,
They're the undefeated,
The ones who, day by day,

Clean the underside of things,
The parts you never see,
The ones who take in breakdowns
And tend them constantly.

MARGARET BARRY
1917–89

She played the streets of Ireland, 'twas her life;
She loved no man but music, so she said;
Her genius, to the Free State, was a knife.

Travelling 'round, a singer, mother, wife,
When Ireland proscribed genius out of dread,
She played the streets of Ireland, 'twas her life,

Where banjo, fiddle, three-card trick and fife
Were moved on by the law's repressive tread.
Her genius, to the Free State, was a knife.

Where was Margaret Barry? Rumours rife:
In Camden town? In Wexford? Was she dead?
She played the streets of Ireland, 'twas her life,

A way she loved despite the pain and strife
That left her with more bedtimes than a bed.
Her genius, to the Free State, was a knife.

I heard her just the once, but lately I've
Been thinking of the music that was bred
To play the streets of Ireland back to life,
Whose genius loosed a free state like a knife.

2

THE DRENCHING NIGHT DRAGS ON

translated from 'Is Fadá Liom Oíche Fhírfhliuch' *by Aogán*
Ó Rathaille (c. 1675–1729)

The drenching night drags on, no sleep, no snore,
Without cattle, sheep, wealth or horned cows in store,
A storm on the sea nearby in my head makes roar,
And I wasn't reared to eating dogfish or winkles by
    the shore.

If the protector-king was living still on the banks of Laune
And his warriors who shared his fate (who'd pity my
    comedown),
If they still ruled this scenic, sheltered, harboured
    coastline 'round,
My family wouldn't be paupers in *Corca Dhuibhne* now.

Fierce, generous MacCarthy, who hated all deceit,
With MacCarthy of the Lee in jail, languid, without
    release,
MacCarthy of Kanturk is dead and all his family –
It bitterly afflicts my heart that they've vanished from
    the scene.

My heart is withered up, my humour's tortured, soured
That the hawks who never penny-pinched, who ruled
    the lands throughout,
From Cashel to *Tonn Cliona*, thence to Thomond should
    have found
Their towns and their great holdings ravaged by the *Gall*.

Oh! wave down here below me, you rant and rave and
   roar,
My brain from your bellowing is distracted, weary, sore.
If help should ever come again to Ireland's lovely shore,
I'd shove your hoarse, harsh howling down your throat.

Corca Dhuibhne: the Dingle Peninsula, County Kerry
Tonn Cliona: Glandore Bay, County Cork
Gall: foreigners, foreign invaders

DÓNALL ÓG

*a translation of the Gaelic folk song 'Dónall Óg',
author unknown*

Dónall Óg, if you cross the ocean,
Take me with you and don't forget,
On fair day and market you'll have a present
And a Greek king's daughter in your bed.

But if you leave, I have your description:
Two green eyes and a fair-haired poll,
A dozen plaits in your yellow ringlets,
Like a cowslip or a garden rose.

Late last night, the dog announced you
And the snipe announced you in the marsh that's deep,
While all alone you walked the woodlands –
May you be wifeless till you find me.

You made a promise, but a lie you told me,
That you'd be before me at the fold;
I gave a whistle and three hundred calls for you
But a bleating lamb your absence told.

You promised me, and it wasn't easy,
Silver masts and a golden fleet,
A dozen towns and all with markets
And a lime-white mansion by the sea.

You promised me and it impossible,
You'd give me gloves made from skin of fish,
You'd give me shoes made out of bird-skin
And a suit made of the dearest silk.

With me, Dónall, you'd do far better
Than with a haughty lady puffed with pride;
I'd milk your cows and I'd do your churning
And I'd strike a blow for you at your side.

Oh my grief! And it isn't hunger,
Lack of food or drink or sleep
That leaves me here so thin and haggard,
But from a young man's love that I am sick.

I saw the youth in the morning early
On horseback riding down the road,
But he didn't approach or entertain me;
I cried my fill as I turned for home.

When I go to the Well of Sorrows
I sit down and wail and sigh
When I see them all there but my darling,
With the amber shadow on his cheekbone high.

'Twas on a Sunday my love I gave you,
The one before last Easter Day,
I on my knees as I read the Passion
But my two eyes gave my love away.

'Don't speak with him,' my mother warned me,
'Today, tomorrow or any day.'
A fine time, now, to give such warning,
Locking the stable when the thief's away.

I beg you, mother, give me to him
And give him all in the world you own,
Even if you have to beg for alms,
But don't deny what I implore.

This heart of mine is black as sloes are,
Black as a coal is in a forge,
Or the print of a shoe in the whitest hall is,
And above my laughter, my heart is sore.

You took my East from me, you took my West,
Before and after I've lost to you,
You took the sun from me, you took the moon,
And I fear you've taken my God too.

THE BOG-DEAL BOARD

a translation of the Gaelic folk song 'An Clár Bog Déil',
author unknown

I'd wed you, join without cow or coin
Or dowry too,
My own! My life! With your parents' consent,
If it so pleased you;
I'm sick at heart that we are not,
You who make my heart to soar,
In Cashel of Munster with nothing under us
But a bog-deal board.

Walk, my love, and come with me
Away to the glen,
And you'll find shelter, fresh air by the river
And a flock bed;
Beneath the trees, beside us
The streams will rush,
The blackbird we'll have for company
And the brown song-thrush.

The love of my heart I gave you –
In secret too;
Should it happen in the course of life
That I and you
Have the holy bond between us
And the ring that's true,
Then if I saw you, love, with another,
I'd die of grief for you.

DONNCHÁ BÁN

a translation of the Gaelic folk song 'Donncha Bán',
author unknown

It was in this town you saw the amazement
On Donncha Bán when he was sentenced,
A white cap on him in place of a hat
And a hempen rope for a cravat.

Through the night without rest or sleep
I've come like a lamb through droves of sheep,
My bosom open, my hair let loose
To find my brother had met the noose.

By the top of the lake I mourned you first,
The second time at the gallows' foot,
The third time above your corpse
Among strangers, my head splitting.

And if I had you back among your own
Down in Sligo or Ballinrobe,
They'd smash the gallows, cut the rope
And send Donncha home by the way he knows.

Donncha Bán, you weren't meant for hanging
But to go to the barn for a spell of threshing,
To turn your plough to right and left
And lift the sod with the red side up.

And Donncha Bán, my brother dear,
Well I know who lured you from here,
They drink their drinks, they light their pipes,
They walk the dew in the dead of night.

And Donncha Bán, it's my great torment,
How well you'd wear the boots and spurs!
I'd dress you in fashions of enduring raiment
And send you out like a great man's son!

Coming home now is your dowry
And it isn't cattle, sheep or horses
But tobacco, pipes and the whitest candles
And I don't begrudge them to all who mourn you.

The Women's Christmas Eve

a translation of 'Oíche Nollaig na mBan' *by Seán Ó Ríordáin (1917–77)*

The storm escaped with a fury last night
(Last night was the Women's Christmas Eve)
From the desolate bedlam that's concealed by the moon
Through the sky, like a madman it screeched
Till my neighbours' gates grated like gaggling geese,
Till the river's wheeze bellowed, a bull,
Till my candle was quenched like a blow to my mouth
That reddened my anger in full.

I'd like that a storm would blow up like that
The night that I'm weakening, and fail,
Going back home from the great dance of life
And the light of sin on the wane;
That each moment be filled with shouts from the sky,
That the world be one screaming mass,
So I won't hear the silence approaching my way
Or the engine of the car as it stops.

The Road of No Returning

a translation of 'An Bealach nach bhFilleann' *by Cathal Ó Searcaigh (b. 1956)*

Here there is no cairn or sign
Or milestone on display
As you enter the desert
To point you on your way.

The naked way of loneliness:
That's the way you'll walk
Alone and in darkness,
Without light from moon or star,
With nothing in store for you
But to stray and wander far . . .

And you won't erect a cairn
Or sign for any who,
Brother, might come after,
As a gust of wind removes
Every last trace
Of the footprints you left this moment
Barely in this place . . .

SONG

a translation of 'Amhrán' *by Cathal Ó Searcaigh*

Don't come with the total truth.
Sweeter far,
my love, to me
is a small ray of solace.

Don't come with the high tide.
All I want is
a cup of well water
to slake my thirst.

Don't come with the whole sky,
with moon and stars.
All I need, love,
is the embers' faint light.

But as a bird carries
drops of water in its feathers,
or as the wind carries
grains of salt from the shore

Come to me always
with a tiny spark, a tear.
A little is all I need
if it comes from your heart, my dear.

3

I Have Seen Great People in My Time

I have seen great people in my time
(Not the kind that aspire to celebrity);
Their great endurance stands up in my rhyme:
They pass the crucial test of poetry.
Only love can see these people thus –
They drink, they fight, they bitch, they fornicate,
They test my vision with their spleen and lust.
Only love survives a loss of faith;
And so I don't give up, they carry on:
We carry on – we have no other choice.
Tomorrow we might all burst into song,
Though nothing's changed, as singers find their voice.
We carry on, often without hope.
Where celebrity would baulk, these people cope.

MOYVANE

Am I reading you, my native place, all wrong?
In reading you, is it myself I read?
Is the village I have turned into song
Real only as a figment of my need?
The characters I see, to other eyes
Are bogmen at home only in a drain
(What do critics do but criticise?);
They survive their critics just the same.

Which is real? I ask myself again;
Is insight a reflection of oneself?
What I make eventually of Moyvane
Is what I make eventually of myself.
What I am depends on what I see
As vision proves itself in poetry.

A Child's Portrait of Jesus

'May the Force be with you,' his Jesus says;
Brainwashed by television, thus he writes.
Brainwashed by television, the games he plays
Are 'Aliens' and such. This isn't right . . .
Hear me at nearly fifty giving out
That the world isn't as it used to be:
Another step, and all our youth are louts.
(Once I dreamed, like them, of being free.)
The world is too much with me. My concern
Robs me of all joy in those I teach:
Like those kids, I too have much to learn,
But I'm at the age when men switch off and preach.
I vent, like the Apostles, adult care.
'Become a child,' the Lord says, 'if you dare.'

I AND THE VILLAGE

A trap, a hay-cart and an empty street
(An image that I've carried all these years),
A greyhound at the corner where we'd meet –
A picture of the past, too deep for sneers.
Jimmy Nolan took that photo way back when
His camera was the only one around.
The village of my childhood. Once again
I'm a child, and this, my native ground,
Is empty as a Sunday afternoon
When pubs are closed and all are at the match;
I sit at Brosnan's Corner on my own,
Empty as the street where I keep watch –
An emptiness he pictured like a poem;
An inward street: the street that leads to home.

THE VOICE

homage to Micheál O'Hehir

What county did he come from? We never knew.
All we knew of him was in his voice;
Everything it told us, we took as true.
He was our Sunday; he was the people's choice,
Our inspiration in a humdrum place;
He raised men up to greatness with his words;
Pre-TV, we never saw his face,
The voice of the young republic; but we heard.

A 'fifties stay-home-Sunday afternoon,
We gather 'round the radio for the match
As Ireland becomes a parish in such rooms . . .
No voice but John McCormack's was a patch
On the voice that brought us visions on the air
As we turned on, tuned in to Micheál O'Hehir.

THE MEADES

Oh, that first night the Meades came to Moyvane!
A pub band with vocals, organ, drums,
The first such band that came here; they'd no van –
Just the leader's car with speaker, microphone,
Drums and organ loaded in the boot.
They'd come from the next village – up from Glin,
Dressed in Sunday best, no flashy suits,
A staid and sober band that drew us in.
Now Mikey Stack takes off his trusty cap
And sings for us (he's never sung before),
And husbands waltz with wives while single chaps
Tear into comely maidens round the floor.
A sleeping village woke the night they came.
Nothing after would ever be the same.

COUNTRY LIFE

It's not so much that I'm out of fashion –
It's more that what I do was never 'in';
Oh sure, they paid lip-service, doled out rations
In some pie-eyed back-to-basics Gaelic dream.
And yes, we're still surviving, dancing, singing
At the crossroads where our betters turned away.
We choose to make a life here while they're clinging
To a past that we who live here know is fey.
And yes! They come on visits to the country
To see a past they say we should 'preserve',
As if we country folk were merely sentries:
When they come back, they get what they deserve –
A place that they no longer recognize,
A progress that they, tourists, must despise.

On Declining a Commission to Write Two-hundred-word Biographies of Irish Writers for Their Portraits in a Hotel

They put the writers' portraits on the wall –
It fills a space and elevates the tone;
Later, they might hold a festival –
No matter that the writers wrote alone.
Everyone is at it, shops, hotels;
'It brings in tourists' seems to be the ploy;
Like wallpaper, it suits the decor well,
And when the tourists come, we know they'll buy
Aran sweaters, crystal, Celtic kitsch,
Harmless stuff that tourists take away
(Budget stuff, upmarket for the rich)
To remind them of their Irish holiday.
They've the writers where they want them – on the wall –
Backdrop to the muzak in the mall.

Scorn Not the Ballad

Scorn not the ballad: it's the tale
Of lives like ours (and told without a fuss).
Sing it with a glass of flowing ale!
What's ours belongs to none, and all, of us.
No other verse can sing us like it does,
No other verse can wring out of the past
The strange, familiar melody that flows
Like truth from all who raise the singing glass.
Scorn not the ballad! Sing it out
In every public house, in every street;
It wasn't made for parlours – hear it shout!
Though sober as a sonnet, hear it beat.
You can't escape its rhythm, rough and rude;
You hum along, not caring if you should.

I Don't Care If What You Sing Is Shite

I don't care if what you sing is shite,
There's more than words will make this world worthwhile;
What offends by day will sing at night
As day resolves itself. In a moment I'll
Be asked to sing a song and then I'll strive
To sing something that the drinkers all will know –
The kind of song that keeps this pub alive,
A poetry that never fails to show
A people who are sung, and thus exist
In a song-line where a melody will bring
What words alone cannot to those who're pissed,
The kind of song we all half-know and sing.
You know us by the songs we sing at night,
The sentiments we keep by day from sight.

IN THE DARK

for John Mole

Evenings Jimmy Mac and his wife Jo
Would sit in their own kitchen after dark
In the silence of true peace. No radio
Disturbed them and if outside a dog would bark,
The peace inside was multiplied. No light
Was turned on; they both would sit content
As darkness fell and twilight turned to night;
This was a house that knew what darkness meant.
If light draws moths to brilliance, then the dark
Drew ramblers to that kitchen, old and young;
Out of the glare, these night-souls would embark,
To find within themselves the source of song,
That bypassed place that opens up at night
With fireside songs that don't survive the light.

TO PÁDRAIG PEARSE

for Declan Kiberd

I see you, Pearse, in Dublin with your sword –
Cuchulainn (hardly!), a poser with a dream.
In the new State, our teachers often bored
Us pink with 'Ireland – How She'd Seem
To Pádraig Pearse'. I didn't give a damn –
Those essays were for old men to offload
Their hang-ups at new freedom. Pearse the man
Was never taught us – teachers toed
The party line in everything they taught;
A poet like Pearse was dangerous, and so
They cast him as our conscience, and some bought
It. I didn't want to know.
They forged you in their image, and I sought
A way to write those essays and to grow.

For George Szirtes

Timmy Halpin holds me with his eye,
Tells me how in nineteen forty-one
(He doesn't want his anecdote to die)
He witnessed isolation in Moyvane.
Jane Hanafin, a woman of the shawl,
Calls into a bar-grocery for tea
(It's not so much that she drank tea at all –
'Twas for kinfolk who might come from overseas);
The publican refuses her request,
He apologises to her from the bar,
'I'm sorry,' he says, guarding the tea chest,
'Tea is rationed now that there's the War.'
'What war?' she asks. She hasn't heard the news,
While in Auschwitz, George, your grandad's gassed, a Jew.

THE HEROES OF MY CHILDHOOD

The heroes of my childhood are unsound:
Age has brought amnesia, and the fact
Is lost, irretrievable in a mind
That makes a gallous fiction of the act.
The old men all are heroes in their own
Stories that they tell me of the past;
I listen, for respect must still be shown –
The men who built this State are dying fast.
Tradition tells us what we need to know,
The truth that can't be proved about ourselves;
I listen well, observe tradition grow
Vital and unsound as old men's tales –
Such stories as have made us what we are:
For this we live and die and go to war.

gallous: a composite word incorporating 'gallant', 'callous'
and 'gallows'

ALZHEIMER'S DISEASE

'They're hanging me this evening,' Mary says,
Or else it's a transplant she must have,
But her concern's observing the Fast Days
(The cares of childhood follow to the grave).
'Am I going to Mass on Sundays?' she repeats
(How the good are frightened of their Church);
All we can do is comfort with deceit.
She's satisfied, and then begins to search
For biscuits, the indulgence of her life –
She'd eat them by the packet were she let,
A humble and obedient country wife;
Everything we tell her she'll forget,
But not the past – the past is as today,
Where she was damned unless she would obey.

LASSIE

At ninety years he fell into a drain –
That's what John Bradley tells me from his bed
(Hospital plays tricks on old men's brains);
But for his dog, he tells me, he'd be dead.
How fact and fiction make us what we are –
He fell at home at bedtime in the dark
(The drain was years ago outside a bar);
His faithful dog had more sense than to bark –
She lay down on her master all night long,
Licked his face and wrapped him from the cold,
And when the ambulance came to take out John,
Lassie stayed and couldn't be consoled.
She guards his house and lets no stranger through –
When there's nothing left, love finds such things to do.

To a Guitar

Frowned upon by purists: rightly so –
So many have done violence to the tune;
Playing you, I've learned all I know
Of music – how it can raise or ruin.
I've seen men take up the fiddle and destroy
Everything they have in music's thrall,
For music's not a thing that we enjoy –
It's a gift that, once it's granted, takes all.
In giving all, we risk all that we are,
There's no hiding when you play a jig or reel
(Even if you're strumming a guitar) –
You're nothing there but what you think and feel.
And it's worth it to make music, take that chance.
You're, either way, a partner in the dance.

THE TENTH STATION OF THE CROSS:
JESUS IS STRIPPED OF HIS GARMENTS

Now, My Lord, you've reached your destiny.
You're stripped of all your garments, and they toss
For the coat they won't make parts of, while we
Make crude and gruesome jokes below the Cross.
Now, My Lord, you're naked and we see
The wounds we have inflicted on your skin.
And still, even here on Calvary,
We sinners can't admit to this, our sin.
Strip me, Lord, till I, like you, am bare,
Till all I am is naked before you;
Then, My Lord, maybe then my prayer
Will be naked as you are, and as true.
Strip me of my garments, that my words
Might be worthy of your life and death, My Lord.

Knockanure Church

A place of worship, simple and austere;
'Sixties architecture past its date.
I wonder what it is that draws me here
To a building local people seem to hate.
The church of their affection, knocked, made way
For the 'garage on the hill' in its design –
Bare brick, flat roof, no steeple, here I pray.
The spirit of this building's kin to mine.

My God's a God who strips me in this place –
No cover here, the lines are stark and spare.
Through the years, I've grown into this space
Where work of human hands raised art to prayer –
The same the builders raised up once at Chartres,
But plainer here, an answer to my heart.

THE MORTUARY CARD

The snaps we use are chosen for their smiles –
No frown will mar the memory of the dead;
And so, the one that's chosen from the piles
Of old photos is chosen for the head
And shoulders. Cut out from the group
(A wedding, perhaps, carnation in lapel),
Without his cap, before old age and stoop,
We see the man we want to see. We tell
Ourselves that this is how he looked in life:
Usually he didn't, but so what?
Useless to plead with daughters, sons or wife
To show him as he was, for what is caught
In the photo on the card his loved ones show
Is the man that doesn't die, the soul they know.

IN MEMORY OF MY FATHER

Since my father died, I've changed. It seems
That I become my father more and more;
I carry him around, awake, in dreams
Who followed me alive. Now his door
Is locked. House closed, I have my father's key;
I open the familiar, room by room –
Not just a house, it's more a memory.
The house itself must not become a tomb,
So I open up the windows, light the fire,
Decide which clothes I'll give to charity
(The rest I'll burn later in a pyre),
Host a farewell for the family
Who share in this last supper, wine and bread,
Who resurrect the memory of the dead.

THE SOLITARY DIGGER

after Paul Henry
in memoriam Sister Anna Danaher

Not a spire in sight but thatch and hay.
She pauses from her digging. All alone,
She digs out good potatoes from the clay.
She'll fear no winter when the work is done.
The crop is good. She pauses for a rest –
No famine now will skeleton the land;
A simple faith submits that God knows best –
There are things she knows she needn't understand.
Just a simple peasant standing with her spade,
Knowing through her hands the fertile earth
In a landscape with not a tree for shade –
This land is hers by labour and by birth.
She pauses from her digging; there is time
To compose oneself where heaven and nature rhyme.

A Corner Boy

'Take therefore no thought for the morrow: for the
morrow shall take thought for the things of itself.
Sufficient unto the day is the evil thereof.'

The Sermon on the Mount

Just lazing at the cross with friends and neighbours,
Just gossiping the morning hours away,
Returning to the time when we, teenagers,
Learned to stand and wait, an idle day
When dogs curled up and slept at Brosnan's Corner,
When our lives stretched out before us like a haze,
When everything seemed happier and warmer –
Ah yes! Those were the very best of days.
And here I am again at Brosnan's Corner
Gossiping the morning hours away.
No! The past was neither happier nor warmer –
Sufficient is its evil to the day.
I stand here with my back against the wall,
Take no thought for a world in its own thrall.

You Trust Me When I Leave You
for the Wild

for Brenda

You trust me when I leave you for the wild –
The poetry, the pub, the after-hours,
The kind of trust that often is defiled
By love betrayed and guilt's false gift of flowers.
My life's a search for poetry; but you,
Content to know the word's not certain good,
Brenda, are everything I know that's true,
While I, your poet, am volatile as mood.
I leave you for the wild, you go to sleep –
I come home late, my head pub-full of lore;
I go down to our room, pull up the sheet
And duvet round your shoulders; then sit more.
You trust me, no matter where I go,
With a trust (it's said) that only children know.

A Sonnet for My Wife

My love will take no bullshit; not from me.
She knows me well, especially when I try
To tint with roses everything I see:
She knows it's self-deception: that I lie.
No! My love grows roses that are real –
The ones you plant and care for all your life,
Blossoms that we both can smell and feel,
Blossoms that I pluck for you, my wife.
And when the black spots come, the roses' blight,
Collapsing self-deception, your belief
Will not give up, as I, without a fight:
You tend the rose and bring it love's relief.
No! My love will take no bullshit, for she knows
That tinted love will not support a rose.

DOUBLE PORTRAIT AU VERRE DE VIN

after Marc Chagall
for Brenda

She takes him on her shoulders; he is light
As the angel that descends about his head;
Mounted on her shoulders, all is bright
(Long enough he's lived among the dead).
He sits upon her shoulders; he is light
As the wine he raises in the glass is red;
Man and wife – no! lovers: in the night
He'll pour himself into her on their bed.
She takes him on her shoulders; dressed in white –
This is the dress she wore the day they wed;
She raises up her love to such a height
He sees the angels dance about his head.
She takes him on her shoulders; he is light.
Mounted on her shoulders, all is bright.